lemon, egg, bread

laura elliott

when you started painting class
you had to do a lemon still life and
you graduated to a lemon and bread
still life and you graduated to a
lemon, egg, bread still life and this
was not my idea of painting

eva hesse

you loved the surreal
the song
the edible
and, above all,
bread.

maggie o'sullivan, *elegy*

for j.r. with love

melon rinds
I mistook
for scraped-out
salmon skins
sugared figs
and jelly sweets
a table that
looks like a bed
scattered with
star anise and
walnut casings
some women
wear so much
makeup
you can smell
their eyelids
but not me
lucky if you can
sense me with
your best organs

did you measure
the water its heart
of silver its inference
of spotlights
I was not dressed yet
but under the window
a horizontal blanket
to cover the splinters
honey cereal sewn
to the bib
yellow plums and
petals dip your hand
inside me
blind watermedia
hollow me out

what does it mean
to go to the coast
and sit facing away
from the sea
the tasting notes
indicate sherry
I used to be able
to draw a great
crested grebe with
quite a high level
of competency
or at least
hegemonic fluency

coconut
shredded
against
the wishes
of a parent
directly onto
the carpet
is pure
topology

a home altar
is a beautiful
necessity
a space apart
for bark
and the inert
utensils

I am not talking
to you said
the neighbour
I am talking to
my neighbour
and slammed
the bathroom
window shut
what is the difference
between a felon
and a villain
or remembering
whether or not
he had an accent
you should be
ashamed of yourself

the largest cave in
the world can fit
the entire new york
skyline in it but
is it hygienic to
share lipsticks or
is it preferable to
sleep all morning

cells of
a carved
blood orange
clung to
the pith
like jammy
fish eggs

face creams again
soften the aspect
and again the
elocutionary
confidence of
scholarly politics
defeats me
I understand
yet I have no
questions not
this time still
maybe warm up
in the bar
oh no wait
hypoglycemic
catastrophe
all the carefully
prepared speeches
have fallen
on the floor
with my sugars

having been devoured
I elaborate
on the pastry
display cases
the mucilaginous
leftovers
always already
consumed
meet myself
across the buffet table
opaque and sombre
as a chin

a room has been
established within which
systems of gift giving
have turned into loans
the tall blue water jug
was a favourite object
of cezanne's

such wastes
drop it is
a repulsively
precocious gift
the distance
between the plate
and the page
a pleated
cotton napkin
a very plain
very un-
extraordinary
lancing

lip on lip
tucked up
in its own
significance
rutting knot
of awe

dross segmented
artichoke hearts
itchy anus and
horror at
the concept
of stones put
inside girls by
men who went
to prison or
of speaking to
your father inside
the clock tower
about robert
mapplethorpe
and I do not
mean his pistils

everything in this
one is all wrong
the moulded
flan the smashed
green glass the wine
stain on the tablecloth
like blood and all
the implications
that come along
with that

get them out
of the suitcase
and put them up
the red flowers
dried and hung
by their ankles
tomatoes musting
the beechwood
like filthy cats'
red petticoats
cut them open!
cut them down!

waiting for
a response
to a letter I haven't
yet posted
sleek linoleum leaves
I ought to
sponge down
but we are both
too stubborn
when I was 18
months old
I refused to walk
anywhere
and the hospital
could find no cause
for this paralysis
except that my first
sister had just been
born and it was all
I could do
not to run for it

coffee cups and
radish-tinted kinks
in a discarded bouquet
cherry stalks crease
the olive linoleum
the pocked and
snowy linen would
you care for a pink
or a green glass
drink what do you
think of the general
specifics of such
recursive instances

little pill on the
one-way mirror
don't tut
or I'll hex bitch
goose hiss

the weekend's
whole brass
armoury
of old country
roses is one
surface beaten
over another
in an eternal
lunar couture

when there was
a moment
I was
finally alone
it was
obscene

lucid eucalyptus
dream-state ok
the flatbed picture-
plane is amber
as a cough
sweet vodka

we who are so multiple
perpetually anticipate
tragedy as a crack
in the wrong direction
there are some words
I have only read
and cannot pronounce
aloud but that does
not mean I lack them

the day they forgot
the flesh
was goat butter
on ice
labneh balls
at the picket lines

just another dusk
we don't touch
barely seasonal
pith and instinct
heel of battenberg
self-archiving
saturation is a
sack of raisins
and here they are
all drowning

everybody's washing-up
pile is sculptural everyone's
abandoned dining table
glued together is an event
like the hollow grey egg
of an 83rd birthday

but old men
eating alone
make me sad
as a wedge

at this angle
there is little
or no distinction
between the table
and the wall
a knot of dill
tumbleweed in
a shell of grease-
proof paper
holds its own
moonstone
atmosphere

newsprint wrapped
around a stale loaf
the cabbage leaf tureen
your mother gave me
in embarrassment
the gnawing
dismemberment
of peach wax tapers
in a room with a draught
was a thursday

why have you
put an onion
in the fridge
oh I see
sex obviously
the concentration
of a woman alone
'the interpolations
of every book
in all books'
the vinegar
cavern

what is that
subtle deflation
that sponge
crumb bomb
deconstructed
cornflower feathers
teased through
the cheesecloth
persistence is
a man on the roof
and it's getting
colder

less interested in
my interests more
interested in making
lists and watching
the solar-powered
crystal lotus in
the window of the
furniture shop
rotate white
hot inedible

exponential gumballs on
the cockled cloth the
oyster-lipped trifle dish
now and then suckling
what is worse to accept
the glut of grey literature
the grainy net of under-
garments the romantic
uncertainties of meat

but to fill in the gaps
my god
who has the time
let the land snails
kern all over

more
or no
less
salt
forever

connotations of
purple may include
menopausal
women's hair
moist muffin
chambers
shiny sharkskin
suits blood
look at this finger
I scratched
bleach into it

flood of ginseng
marzipan sheeting
baking is a pastime
much like drinking
a duration of time
in which one warms
and sweetens before
the madeira belly
of it all caves in

only one person
asked a question
it was about women
appearing and
men acting and
no one really did
anything to stop
him from deflecting
the question
yet distracted as
I am by staircases
the shame was mine

I'm going to take
a shit about it
in the sterile
cell I call
your name
out

what am I supposed
to say tessellated
cucumber tiles
ice bark beakers
a milk bottle cap in
the centre of a siren light
all the pedagogical
inaccuracies of hindsight

acid tangerine
in the throat
of a turquoise vase
faithless
citrus
glottal-stop

I noticed the way
she colours the edges
of the wood to reflect
onto the whitewash
and emanate neon
not that neon alone
is glorious but an
effort to harness
a glow like that is
positively geological

lemonade is devastating
I mean derivative I
mean the difference
between us is that
you hoped to one day
meet them and I had
no idea they still existed

and figs were new
until they
weren't anymore
and jackfruits
and persimmons
and rosehip tea
in a dictionary
of antique
glass I found
the name for
a sensitive
woman overcome
by screaming

you are the
cultural
evangelist
of my
metabolism
bring me
once-fresh
garlands
from temple
steps

isosceles light
striations
on the terrible
sage
the afternoon
goes on
disembowelling

watch the entrails
twitch
it is some kind
of song
some kind of
vibration
on the earth
I can't
not allow

spinach towelette
beside the mirrored
finger bowl
disconcerting broth
of intervals

the ornamental
appetite
is a still life
longing
for organs

lemon, egg, bread by Laura Elliott. Published (ISBN 978-0-9935693-6-4) by Test Centre in 2017 in an edition of 300 copies, with drawings by Florence Shaw. Designed by Traven T. Croves and printed by Unicum, Netherlands. Copyright © Laura Elliott 2017. All rights reserved. No part of this publication may be reproduced, stored in a retrieval system, or transmitted, in any form or by any means, electronic, mechanical, photocopying, recording or otherwise, without the prior permission of the publishers. A CIP record for this book is available from the British Library. Test Centre Publications, 71 Oriel Road, London, E9 5SG / www.testcentre.org.uk.